THE FIELD GUIDE TO
RAIN FOREST
ANIMALS

by Nancy Honovich

Silver Dolphin

Silver Dolphin Books
An imprint of the Advantage Publishers Group
5880 Oberlin Drive, San Diego, CA 92121-4794
www.silverdolphinbooks.com

The Field Guide to Rain Forest Animals is produced by becker&mayer!,
Bellevue, Washington
www.beckermayer.com

If you have any questions or comments about this product, please visit
www.beckermayer.com/customerservice.html and click on Customer Service Request Form.

ISBN-13: 978-1-59223-719-7
ISBN-10: 1-59223-719-3

Printed, manufactured, and assembled in China.

1 2 3 4 5   11 10 09 08 07

07364

Written by Nancy Honovich
Edited by Ben Grossblatt
Designed by Ryan Hobson and Eddee Helms
Illustrated by Marc Dando and Ryan Hobson
Paper models and dioramas designed and illustrated by Ryan Hobson, assisted by Christine Lee
Production management by Katie Stephens
Photo research by Zena Chew

Greetings!

My name is Harold Bennington, and I have just returned from the depths of the Amazon rain forest in South America, where I spent several weeks on a research expedition funded by the Charles Natural History Museum. Covering an area of more than 2 million square miles, the Amazon is the world's largest rain forest and the home of thousands of different plant and animal species, many of which have yet to be discovered. Observing the area's beautiful and dangerous wildlife up close was a fascinating, enlightening, and powerful experience.

The officials of the Charles Natural History Museum were eager to introduce the mysterious animals of the Amazon rain forest to the museum's visitors, so I kept a notebook of my observations while I was in the field. In addition, I created models of eight of the amazing creatures I encountered on my travels.

As you read through my notebook, you can assemble the models and imagine that you are with me on my expedition in the unknown depths of the Amazon.

Harold Bennington

May 1, 1924

Jaguar
Panthera onca

March 3, 1924—State of Amazonas, Brazil

Two days ago, my guide Don Gilberto and I arrived in Brazil. Yesterday, we plowed through the dense vegetation around Envira searching for any sign of the ferocious jaguar. At nightfall, our patience was rewarded. While examining a set of scratches carved into a tree, our attention was diverted by the sound of rustling leaves coming from above. When I looked up, I spied a cat with the stocky build of a pit bull creeping slowly across a branch. As the animal leaped to the ground, Don Gilberto nudged me into a thicket of bushes so that we could observe the animal.

Brownish-yellow fur with dark markings.

Eyes are a golden-reddish brown.

Broad head.

To the native people of Central and South America, the jaguar is a symbol of power. It is associated with thunder, lightning, and rain. Various cultures of the region pay homage to this animal by depicting it on masks and statues.

Long, curved retractable claws.

Assembly

The jaguar pieces are marked
as in the diagram below:

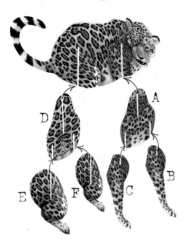

Your finished jaguar:

Quick Attack

The jaguar had not detected us, but was instead interested in a three-banded armadillo about 15 feet away. We watched as the jaguar pounced on the unsuspecting animal. What an attack! Most animals would shy away from the armadillo because its armored shell is hard to penetrate. But the jaguar had no such problem. Using its sharp claws to hold its struggling prey, the jaguar sank its teeth into the armadillo's skull and shell.

Ready to attack!

Unsuspecting
armadillo

Water Cat

Most cats are not known for their swimming ability, much less a love of water. But the jaguar is an exception. I caught sight of one jaguar swimming across a stretch of water that must have measured a half a mile in length!

Notes on communication

• Jaguars are loners in the animal world. When faced with another jaguar, this fierce cat will grunt and growl as if to say, "Step back!"

• Though the jaguar is able to grunt and growl, I have not heard it roar as most large cats do. Its roar is more like a loud cough than a full-throated roar.

• A jaguar often urinates on trees to mark its territory. When another animal gets a whiff of the scent, it knows to stay away.

• Jaguars sharpen their deadly claws by scratching trees. The scratch marks also help mark the jaguar's territory.

Jungle Shadow

One day I spotted a big cat that looked like a jaguar, but was all black. When I looked through my binoculars, I saw that it was indeed a jaguar, and that it only appeared all black. The rosettes and spots were still visible under the cat's yellowish-black coat. Don Gilberto says we were lucky to spot the black jaguar (what some people call a black panther) because few jaguars are born with this genetic variation.

To the Trees

Over the past few days I have been fortunate enough to observe more of these mysterious wild cats. When it isn't hunting, the jaguar will spend the day bathing in the river or in streams—most likely to cool off from the Amazon's warm, humid climate. Jaguars can also be found resting on tree branches as high as the rain forest canopy.

Jaguars are terrific climbers. They can reach the rain forest canopy, which is about 100 to 130 feet above the ground.

VENEZUELA
GUYANA
COLOMBIA
FRENCH GUIANA
ECUADOR
Amazon River
BRAZIL
PERU
BOLIVIA
CHILE
PARAGUAY
ARGENTINA

N
W E
S

Amazon River
COARI
BRAZIL
ENVIRA
PERU
BOLIVIA

Black eye surrounded by bright yellow eye ring.

Whitish skin around eyes and lower beak.

Deeply hooked beak.

Bright red feathers on back and wing.

Outer toes point backward. Inner toes point forward.

Bright yellow feathers on wing.

Scarlet Macaw

Ara macao

March 9, 1924—Around Coari, Amazonas, Brazil

The Amazon is a noisy place! Close your eyes on any given day and you can hear the squawks, peeps, and chatter of the various bird species that live here. The birds come in many different colors—the most vibrant being the scarlet macaw, which Don Gilberto and I had the privilege of encountering early today.

The scarlet macaw is a member of the parrot family. It measures about 35 inches long and weighs about 2 pounds.

Deep blue feathers on the wing edges.

Tricky Eater

Unripe fruits and nuts tend to contain chemicals that can be toxic. But the scarlet macaw can safely eat unripe nuts. I watched as a macaw used its left foot and beak to grasp one of the many unripe nuts in a tree. With its sharp beak, the macaw crushed the coconut—like shell of the nut almost effortlessly. It quickly devoured the contents before making its way to the next unripe nut.

Assembly

The macaw pieces are marked as in the diagram below:

A

C   B

Your finished macaw:

Feathers

Individual feathers in the wings and tail of a bird play important roles in controlling flight. The tail feathers, like this one, often act as rudders. They help the bird balance and steer as it flies. The scarlet macaw's bright color can make it an easy target for predators such as snakes, toucans, monkeys, and jaguars. But the dense leaves and branches of the rain forest canopy provide the bird with camouflage, making it difficult to spot.

The scarlet macaw was considered sacred by the ancient Mayan civilization. The bird represented daylight and the rising sun.

Nesting

Over the past couple of days, I had observed several macaws flying high into trees. Using a rope and grapple that Don Gilberto was wise enough to bring, I climbed one of the countless trees of the forest. About 100 feet up in the rain forest canopy, I came across a cavity in the tree that looked like it had been hollowed out by termites. Inside the hole, a family of macaws—two adults and four chicks—had built a nest.

Antidote

Early this morning, I witnessed something bizarre: macaws and other bird species descended on a patch of earth along the riverbank and began eating the clay soil! Some observers have suggested that the minerals in the clay somehow act as an antidote, counteracting the toxins in the seeds the birds eat.

Great Escape!

From my perch in the canopy, I heard the chatter of yet another family of macaws coming from the cavity of a nearby tree. I wasn't the only creature in the rain forest canopy to discover them. A python nestled around a branch several yards below also took note and slithered toward the cavity. As the snake inched closer, it rustled a few leaves. The motion alarmed at least one of the adult birds, which emerged and squawked to alarm its family. One by one, the birds flew from their nest, just narrowly escaping the clutches of the hungry snake.

Squirrel Monkey

Saimiri boliviensis

March 16, 1924—Around Borba, Amazonas, Brazil

During my travels through the Amazon, I have encountered dozens of species of monkeys, ranging from the large howler monkey to the pygmy marmoset—a monkey so small it can sit in the palm of your hand. These species all live in the canopy of the rain forest, and I had not witnessed a single one come to the ground—until today. Early this morning I was awakened by a commotion outside my tent. I peeked outside to see two small monkeys scampering across the ground like squirrels. In fact, they were squirrel monkeys.

SOUTH AMERICA

VENEZUELA
COLOMBIA
GUYANA
FRENCH GUIANA
Amazon River
ECUADOR
BRAZIL
PERU
BOLIVIA
CHILE
PARAGUAY
ARGENTINA

N W E S

Amazon River
COARI • • • • BORBA
BRAZIL

Squirrel monkeys are about 12 inches in length.

Gray or olive-colored fur on body.

Dark fur on forehead.

Dark skin around mouth.

Like all monkeys, the squirrel monkey is a type of primate. Primates are mammals that have large brains and forward-looking eyes. Most primates, including squirrel monkeys, have opposable thumbs.

Dexterous fingers with short thumbs.

Nails instead of claws.

New World vs. Old World

The monkeys that live in the Amazon, as well as other parts of South and Central America, are called New World monkeys. Monkeys from Africa, Asia, and Europe are called Old World monkeys. There are several differences between these two groups, but the most noticeable difference is the nose.

The hamadryas baboon is an Old World monkey. Its snout is long and its nostrils are curved and set close together.

The squirrel monkey is a New World monkey. Its snout is short and its nostrils are round and set far apart.

Assembly

The monkey pieces are marked as in the diagram below:

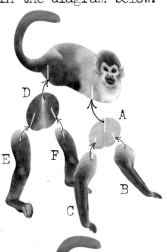

D

E   F

C

A

B

Your finished monkey:

Foraging

For several hours I watched two squirrel monkeys pick fruit, nuts, and berries from nearby bushes and trees. Occasionally, they would use their long fingers to search through the soil and overturn rocks and leaves, on the trail of a tasty prize. They seemed especially fond of grasshoppers.

A squirrel monkey favorite!

The squirrel monkey is an omnivore, or an animal that eats both plants and animals.

Monkey Talk

Squirrel monkeys are very vocal. They have over 25 calls, including chucks, peeps, cackles, and barks. The monkeys call out as they forage, perhaps to keep tabs on each other. The calls also seem to communicate feelings such as anger, affection, and fear. This afternoon, I observed one monkey bark at a hawk, which no doubt wanted to make a meal out of the small, furry creature. The hawk, clearly startled by the sound, flew away!

The Troop

I watched two monkeys abandon the ground and head for the trees. For several minutes they traveled inland, leaping from one branch to another. Finally they reached their home in the trees, where they took their place among a troop that must have consisted of more than 100 members! After some time, I noticed that the troop was divided into three groups, each demonstrating different behaviors.

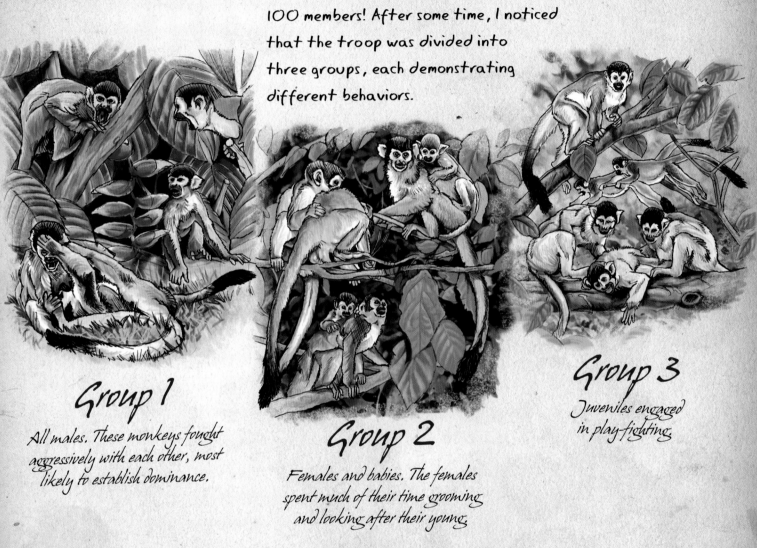

Group 1

All males. These monkeys fought aggressively with each other, most likely to establish dominance.

Group 2

Females and babies. The females spent much of their time grooming and looking after their young.

Group 3

Juveniles engaged in play-fighting.

Scent

I suspect that the squirrel monkey also uses scent to communicate. I saw one monkey urinate on his hands and feet, which he then wiped on other parts of his body. After washing himself in this way, the monkey scurried away from his troop. Moments later, several troop members followed in the same direction. This urine's scent seemed to mark a trail for the others to follow.

VENEZUELA
COLOMBIA
GUYANA
FRENCH GUIANA
ECUADOR
Amazon River
PERU
BRAZIL
BOLIVIA
PARAGUAY
CHILE
ARGENTINA
URUGUAY

N
W E
S

Amazon River
BORBA
PARINTINS
BRAZIL

Tapir

Tapirus terrestris

March 24, 1924—Around Parintins, Amazonas, Brazil

Since arriving in the Amazon, I have stumbled upon some of the most remarkable animals I've ever seen. Today I encountered one of the strangest. Don Gilberto and I were traveling east along the Amazon's muddy bank when we came across a set of freshly made tracks. These three—toed footprints were made by a Brazilian lowland tapir. Moments later, the creature emerged from the forest.

White-rimmed ears

Long, rubbery snout called a proboscis.

Small eyes.

Bulky body covered in gray-brown fur.

Three toes on each back foot.

Four toes on each front foot.

A lowland tapir belongs to an order of animals called Perissodactyla, which means "odd-numbered toes." (The tapir has four toes on each front foot and three toes on each hind foot.) All toes have hooves, and each foot has a callous pad that supports some of the animal's weight. Other perissodactyls are rhinoceroses, horses, and zebras.

Assembly

The tapir pieces are marked as in the diagram below:

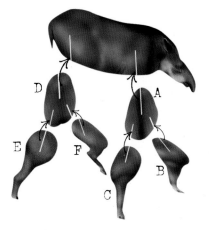

Your finished tapir:

Wallowing

As we drew near I noticed a horde of parasites—including mosquitoes and ticks—swarming about the animal's body. The tapir attempted to brush the pests off with its hooves and snout, but without much success. Clearly fed up, the animal stomped into the muddy water beside the river's bank. Could water soothe the tapir? Don Gilberto and I rolled up our pants and slowly entered the river to find out. We saw schools of fish feeding off the parasites that were latched onto the tapir's skin!

Parasites feed on the tapir's blood. No wonder the tapir is so eager to get rid of these pests!

Big Breath

Water not only helps a tapir remove parasites but also protects the animal from predators. Early this evening, we observed a hungry jaguar pounce on a tapir's back. I thought the animal was doomed, but I was in for a surprise—as was the jaguar. With the wild cat still on its back, the tapir charged into the river until we could see it no more. After a couple of minutes the jaguar surfaced, unable to hold its breath any longer. But there was no sign of the tapir. The jaguar swam to the shore, where it remained for a few moments, pacing back and forth, staring at the water. Still seeing no sign of the tapir, the frustrated jaguar gave up and left. About 10 minutes after the struggle, the tapir emerged from the water. It had saved its own life by holding its breath!

Babies

Unlike adult tapirs, young tapirs have spots and stripes on their coats. These stripes and spots work as camouflage, helping youngsters blend in with the jungle.

A baby tapir grows to full size in 18 months, but stays with its mother for up to four years.

Forest Maker

The lowland tapir is a herbivore. It feeds on a variety of leaves, buds, and branches, which it tears from plants and trees. When a tapir smells an appetizing leaf, it uses its fleshy snout to grab it. As a lowland tapir digests the plants it has eaten, seeds from the plants pass through the animal's digestive tract. The tapir then defecates these seeds in clumped areas known as latrines. Over many years, the seeds germinate and grow into trees. According to Don Gilberto, the lowland tapir is responsible for the growth of many palm trees that grow on Maraca, an island off the coast of northern Brazil.

A tapir's proboscis is a nose, an upper lip, and sometimes a snorkel!

Maternal Bond

One evening I saw a mother and baby tapir foraging for food together. The mother tapir sniffed through the debris on the forest floor, like she was hunting something she could smell but couldn't see. Soon, she found a piece of fruit, and she made a call like a high-pitched whistle to tell her baby to come eat.

Dwarf Caiman

Paleosuchus palpebrosus

March 26, 1924—Obidos, State of Pará, Brazil

As we approached Obidos, Don Gilberto suggested we rent a boat from a local fisherman in order to get a closer look at the region's marine creatures. After boarding a small wooden rowboat fitted with a motor, we headed upriver. We carefully navigated around several sharp rocks jutting above the water's surface. What kind of creature could live in such a rough environment? I was about to find out! About five miles into our journey I noticed a small reptile basking on a jagged rock. I asked Don Gilberto to cut the motor so that we could get a look. As we drifted closer, my guide informed me that we were looking at a Cuvier's dwarf caiman.

Flexible tail.

The Cuvier's dwarf caiman is the smallest crocodilian I have ever seen. This full-grown male was about 5 feet long. That's one-fourth the size of the Australian saltwater crocodile, the world's largest crocodilian.

Partially webbed toes on hind feet.

Red-brown eyes.

Nostrils above snout.

Upper jaw overlaps its lower jaw.

Defense

The caiman pushed itself into the water, and I moved in for a closer look—perhaps too close. The small creature detected my presence and mistook me for an enemy. It raised part of its body above the surface so that it appeared to be standing vertically in the water. It then puffed up its chest and hissed at me. What a spectacle! I decided not to take any chances and gave it some room.

Caiman are at home in the water and can remain under the surface for hours.

Assembly

The caiman pieces are marked as in the diagram below:

Your finished caiman:

21

Built for the Amazon

Surviving in such a harsh environment can't be easy for many animals. But the Cuvier's dwarf caiman appears to be built for the challenge. It is completely covered in bony, armorlike scales. Even its eyelids are bony! In spite of its small size, the Cuvier's dwarf caiman has few predators. That's because its tough skin makes it difficult for most animals to swallow. There are, however, a few creatures that do prey on the caiman: anacondas, boa constrictors, and jaguars.

I discovered these small scales near the caiman I was observing. Unlike many reptiles that molt, or shed their entire skin at once, the caiman appears to shed its scales one at a time.

The leaves of water hyacinths rest above the water. Their feathery roots remain below the surface, where they absorb nutrients.

Hunting

As a Cuvier's dwarf caiman searches for food above the water's surface, it is almost completely submerged in the water. Only its eyes and nostrils remain above the water. The caiman also uses aquatic plants such as water hyacinths to camouflage itself while it hunts.

Crocodilian Snouts

In my travels all over the world, I have noticed that the snouts of different crocodilians vary in width. The wider the snout, the more capable the animal is of seizing larger prey.

Nile Crocodile

Eats fish, turtles, amphibians, and large mammals such as zebras, giraffes, and buffalo. Some Nile crocodiles have been known to eat lions.

Cuvier's Dwarf Caiman

Eats crabs, birds, reptiles, small mammals, and fish.

Indian Gharial

Eats fish.

American Alligator

Eats fish, birds, turtles, amphibians, and mammals such as deer and feral pigs.

Vision

The Cuvier's dwarf caiman is most active at night. Like most nocturnal animals, it has eyes with pupils that open very wide in the dark. This allows as much light as possible into the eye.

SOUTH AMERICA

VENEZUELA
GUYANA
COLOMBIA
Amazon River
BRAZIL
ECUADOR
PERU
BOLIVIA
CHILE
PARAGUAY
ARGENTINA

N W E S

OBIDOS
MANAUS
Amazon River
BRAZIL

Amazon River Dolphin

Inia geoffrensis

March 30, 1924—Manaus, Amazonas, Brazil

Early this rainy morning, we resumed our trip along the Amazon River, now traveling westward. After passing the port of Manaus, we cut the boat's motor and started paddling. During this time I noticed many small channels branching out from the river. As I was considering exploring one of these channels, I felt something tug at my oar. I looked down and saw the culprit's face. "That's an Amazon River dolphin," said Don Gilberto. The animal proceeded to chatter noisily and then used its tail to splash me!

Flukes.

No dorsal fin—just a ridge on its back.

Body is pink, though young dolphins are gray.

Blowhole.

Small eyes.

The Amazon River dolphin (also called a boto) gets its pink color from blood flowing through capillaries located close to the skin's surface.

Large flippers.

Assembly

The dolphin pieces are marked as in the diagram below:

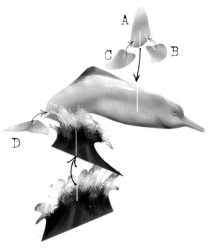

Your finished dolphin:

Flexibility

We watched, amused, as the dolphin navigated its way around the submerged trees. To get a better look, I put on my diving mask and snorkel and dived in. I was amazed by what I saw. Most dolphins have a limited range of motion: they can only move their necks from side to side and up and down. But the Amazon River dolphin is extremely flexible. It can move its neck 180 degrees. This range of motion comes in handy as it weaves around obstacles in the river.

Hunting with Echoes

How can an animal find food in such murky waters? Like other dolphins, the river dolphin must use echolocation. In this process, the dolphin makes a series of clicks that travel through the water until they hit another object or creature. The sound waves then bounce back to the dolphin. This allows the dolphin to gauge where its next meal (or enemy) lies.

Wet Season

We followed our new friend as he traveled away from the main river and into a small channel. As we paddled, I looked at the flooded forest around us. Only six months earlier, one could have explored this area on foot. But during the wet season, rainfall causes the water levels to rise, making the area accessible only by boat.

Breathing

The Amazon River dolphin may be a water-dwelling creature, but it is a mammal. It has lungs—not gills—and therefore must surface to breathe. The dolphin inhales air through a blowhole located on top of its head. When its lungs are filled, a muscular plug closes the blowhole to keep water out. The dolphin then dives into the water, where it can remain for about two minutes. When the dolphin returns to the surface, it makes a short, explosive exhalation before repeating the process for its next dive.

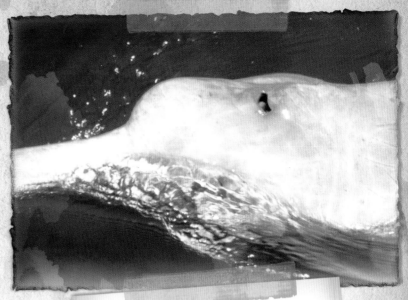

Many native people of the Amazon believe that harming a river dolphin brings bad luck. As a result, it is one of the few animals of the region that is rarely hunted.

Useful Beaks

The Amazon River dolphin's long, narrow beak holds up to 70 teeth in each of its jaws (upper and lower). Their front teeth grab prey and their back teeth crush it. Their beaks are covered with small, stiff bristles. Perhaps these bristles help these dolphins find food in muddy river bottoms.

SOUTH AMERICA

VENEZUELA
COLOMBIA
ECUADOR
Amazon River
PERU
BRAZIL
BOLIVIA
CHILE
PARAGUAY

N
W E
S

COLOMBIA
ECUADOR
MANAUS
Amazon River
PERU   IQUITOS
BRAZIL

Coati

Nasua nasua

April 3, 1924—Iquitos, Peru

We traveled west along the main river until we reached Iquitos, a port in northern Peru. There we met a farmer who offered us lodgings. Eager to sleep in a bed, we graciously accepted the offer and piled into his horse-drawn wagon. Shortly after arriving, the farmer pointed out a papaya tree. We noticed an animal already feasting on one of the fruits. It was a coati.

Brown-gray fur on body.

Pointed snout that's white on the end.

Five toes with claws on each foot.

Ringed tail with long fur.

Coatis, also referred to as coatimundis, are related to raccoons.

28

Fine Noses

The coati uses its excellent sense of smell when searching for food. With its nose to the ground, the animal carefully sniffs leaf litter, rotting logs, and the dirt surface of the forest floor. Today I watched one coati zero in on an insect beneath the ground. Using its claws and long snout, the coati dug into the earth until it uncovered its prey. During the course of the afternoon, I watched the coati find and consume everything from beetles and spiders to frogs and lizards.

Assembly

The coati pieces are marked as in the diagram below:

D

A

E

F

B

C

Your finished coati:

Social Behavior

Just when I was beginning to think that the coati was a solitary creature, I came across a clearing where a large group of coatis was assembled. Like the lone coati I had followed into the forest, they appeared to be scouring the area for food. This noisy band of coatis consisted of five youngsters, seven adult females, and only one adult male. The band appeared to be very close. Occasionally, the females would take a break from foraging to groom each other, while the youngsters would play-fight. During this time the females never lost sight of the young.

Coatis are excellent climbers.

Coatis spend almost all of their waking hours foraging for food.

In addition to foraging, the coati spends quite a bit of time grooming. It uses its incisors to comb its fur and to pull out ticks and burrs.

Food Fights

The young coatis sure are aggressive! I noticed one young male coati digging a small pit in the ground. It was obvious that he was onto something. Sure enough, he pulled a large insect from the pit. Before he had a chance to savor the morsel, another young coati—a female—caught sight of the insect and lunged at the male coati. This was no play-fight! The two coatis struggled for some time before the female pried the insect from the male and devoured it. Throughout the day, I observed many young coatis engage in battles over food. They even lunged at the adults, who actually tolerated the behavior!

Coatis can run faster than 15 miles per hour!

Coati observations:

• When different bands of coatis meet, they generally tolerate each other. Sometimes, they even forage together.

• Play-fighting is important to young mammals. It not only reinforces social bonds but also helps them develop hunting and fighting skills.

• When the juvenile males become adults at two years old, they leave their groups and become solitary.

• During the breeding season, more males temporarily join the group.

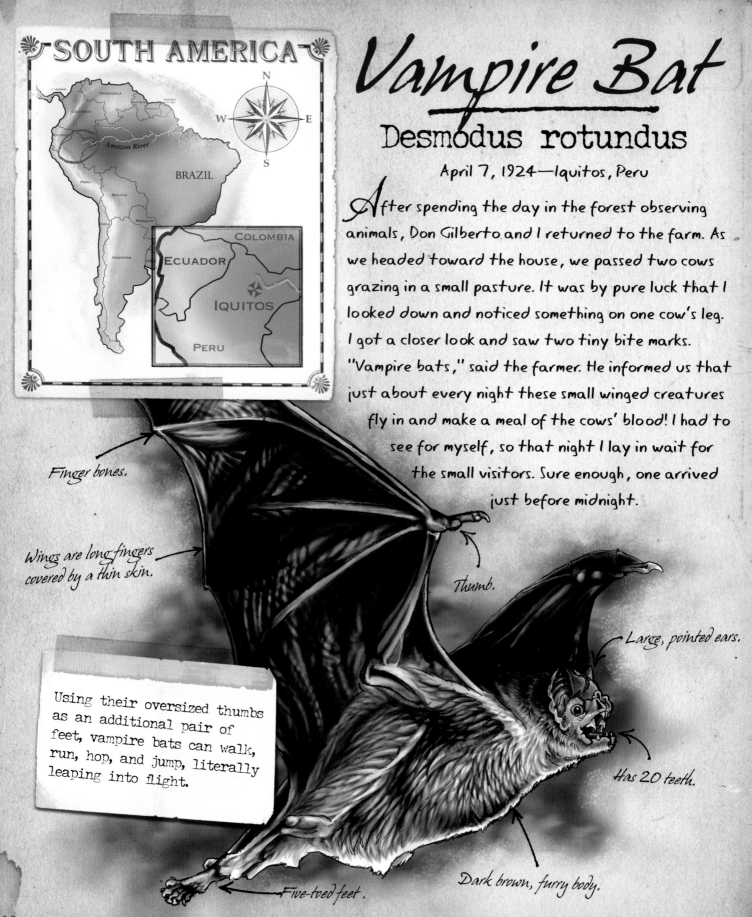

SOUTH AMERICA

N
W — E
S

BRAZIL

Amazon River

PERU

BOLIVIA

PARAGUAY

CHILE

ARGENTINA

VENEZUELA

COLOMBIA

ECUADOR

PANAMA

GUYANA

FRENCH GUIANA

SURINAM

COLOMBIA

ECUADOR

IQUITOS

PERU

Vampire Bat
Desmodus rotundus
April 7, 1924—Iquitos, Peru

After spending the day in the forest observing animals, Don Gilberto and I returned to the farm. As we headed toward the house, we passed two cows grazing in a small pasture. It was by pure luck that I looked down and noticed something on one cow's leg. I got a closer look and saw two tiny bite marks. "Vampire bats," said the farmer. He informed us that just about every night these small winged creatures fly in and make a meal of the cows' blood! I had to see for myself, so that night I lay in wait for the small visitors. Sure enough, one arrived just before midnight.

Finger bones.

Wings are long fingers covered by a thin skin.

Thumb.

Large, pointed ears.

Using their oversized thumbs as an additional pair of feet, vampire bats can walk, run, hop, and jump, literally leaping into flight.

Has 20 teeth.

Dark brown, furry body.

Five-toed feet.

Assembly

The bat pieces are marked as in the diagram below:

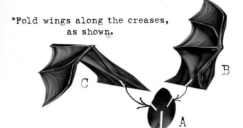

*Fold wings along the creases, as shown.

C

B

A

Your finished bat:

Bats must be able to digest their huge meals quickly. Otherwise, they'd be too heavy to fly away!

The Approach

The bat quietly made its way to the cow, fluttering directly in front of the animal's face. Don Gilberto mentioned that there is an old legend that bats do this to release a tranquilizing scent to keep their victims from waking. However, it's more likely that the bats are taking note of their victim's breathing. This allows them to remember the identity and location of the victim, should they decide to return.

The Pounce

The bat took to the ground and then scuttled—on foot—toward the large animal's rear. As it approached, the sleeping cow jerked its leg. To avoid being hit by the hoof, the vampire bat leaped off the ground. Showing no signs of fear, the bat inched forward and pounced on the cow.

This baby appeared at our campsite.

Baby Bats

Newly born bats are extremely dependent on their mothers. And they don't drink blood! Instead, the newborns feed on their mother's milk. The farmer informed me that this milk diet lasts for about three months. If a young bat is orphaned, other female bats in the colony will adopt it.

The Colony

Early this afternoon, the farmer took us to a cave just down the road. Inside, we found a colony of vampire bats roosting from the ceiling. And they weren't alone—many other bat species were present.

A bat's body is well adapted for hanging upside down. Bats have special tendons that hold their toes in place so that they can cling to their roosts without expending any energy. In fact, bats must flex their muscles in order to let go of the roosting surface.

Homeward Bound

Today marked the end of my great Amazon adventure. Don Gilberto accompanied me to Lima, the capital of Peru, where I caught a ship bound for home. Before I left, I expressed to Don Gilberto my gratitude for his guidance.

This expedition has surpassed all of my expectations. Nowhere else have I encountered such unusual wildlife. From the ferocious jaguar to the colorful, clay-eating scarlet macaw, the Amazon is home to some of the most beautiful creatures in the world.

The information I've gathered will surely aid me in creating an outstanding museum exhibit. I can't wait to tell my colleagues about the lowland tapir that escaped the clutches of a hungry jaguar, and the Amazon River dolphin that skillfully navigated its way around a flooded forest floor.

I am extremely grateful to the Charles Natural History Museum for giving me the opportunity to explore this unforgettable region. I can only hope that I will return one day.

Harold Bennington

Lima, Peru.

Assemble Your Diorama

The first step in assembling your diorama is to carefully punch out the pieces. Then follow the instructions below:

Grove

Fold outward

Waterfall

Fold outward *Fold inward* *Fold inward* *Fold outward* *Fold inward*

Fold outward

Fold outward *Fold inward* *Fold outward* *Fold outward* *Fold outward*

Cave

Fold outward *Fold inward* *Fold outward*

Fold Up *Fold down*

Side view.

Display Your Animals

This is just one example of an assembled diorama. You can set up yours any way you like!